The Library of
HOLIDAYS

Independence Day

Leslie C. Kaplan

The Rosen Publishing Group's
PowerKids Press™
New York

To Ben

Published in 2004 by The Rosen Publishing Group, Inc.
29 East 21st Street, New York, NY 10010

Copyright © in 2004 by The Rosen Publishing Group, Inc.

First Edition

Editor: Jannell Khu

Book Design: Michael J. Caroleo, Michael de Guzman, and Nick Sciacca

Photo Credits: Cover, p. 22 © Ariel Skelley/CORBIS; p. 4 © SuperStock; pp. 7, 11, 12, 16 © Bettmann/CORBIS; p. 8 © CORBIS; pp. 15, 20 © EyeWire/Getty Images; p. 19 © Bill Ross/CORBIS.

Kaplan, Leslie C.
Independence Day / Leslie C. Kaplan.— 1st ed.
     v. cm. — (The library of holidays)
Includes bibliographical references and index.
Contents: What is Independence Day?—Under British rule—War breaks out—The Declaration of Independence—A famous birthday—Another big birthday—Fireworks on the Fourth—The Liberty Bell—Other holiday symbols—Celebrating Independence Day.
  ISBN 0-8239-6663-1 (lib. bdg.)
1. Fourth of July—Juvenile literature. 2. Fourth of July celebrations—Juvenile literature. [1. Fourth of July. 2. Holidays.] I. Title. II. Series.
  E286 .A1383 2004
  394.2634—dc21

                                                                            2002013509

Manufactured in the United States of America

Contents

IN CONGRESS. JULY 4, 1776.

The unanimous Declaration of the thirteen united States of America.

What Is Independence Day?

Americans **celebrate** Independence Day on July 4. It is a day to remember how America gained its freedom from Great Britain. The holiday's date comes from an important event that occurred in 1776. On July 4 of that year, American leaders **adopted** the **Declaration of Independence**. Since then, Americans have celebrated July 4 as the birthday of the United States. Many people spend this holiday outdoors, gathering for parades, picnics, and speeches. At night everyone looks up to see fireworks flash across the sky.

The Declaration of Independence stated that the 13 American colonies wanted to be free from British rule.

Under British Rule

By 1750, there were 13 colonies along the eastern coast of America. The colonists lived far away from Britain, but they remained under British rule. They had to follow British laws. George III, king of Great Britain, ordered the colonists to pay heavy taxes. This angered them. The colonists had no vote in the British government, and felt that the taxes were unfair. By the late 1770s, many colonists in America were no longer **loyal** to the king. They wanted to be free from British rule.

George III sent British soldiers to live among the colonists to make sure that they obeyed his rules. ▶

War Breaks Out

In 1774, the leaders of several colonies met in Philadelphia, Pennsylvania. The meeting was called the First **Continental Congress**. The leaders searched for answers to their problems with Britain. At the Second Continental Congress in 1775, the leaders decided that the colonies must fight for independence. The **American Revolution** broke out in 1775. The American army was not as strong as the British army. Despite this, after many hard battles, the colonists won the war in 1783. The colonies were independent from Britain!

On April 19, 1775, British troops met the Americans in Lexington, Massachusetts, in the first battle of the American Revolution.

The Declaration of Independence

Thomas Jefferson was a leader for the Virginia colony. The Second Continental Congress asked him to write a declaration explaining their ideas. This paper was called the Declaration of Independence. Jefferson wrote that the colonists wanted to be free from British rule to form a new nation, the United States of America. He wrote that everyone has a right to "life, liberty, and the **pursuit** of happiness." Congress, which included men such as Ben Franklin, agreed on the exact wording of the declaration on July 4, 1776.

This painting shows Thomas Jefferson reading the rough draft of the Declaration of Independence to Benjamin Franklin. ▶

An Important Birthday

On July 4, 1876, America had a important birthday. It had been 100 years since America declared independence from Great Britain. To celebrate, the World's Fair was held in Philadelphia. America and 39 other countries **participated**. France had planned to give the **Statue of Liberty** to America as a birthday gift. Only the statue's right arm was ready in time for the fair. Today you can see the completed Statue of Liberty in New York Harbor. Nearly 10 million people had visited the World's Fair by the time it closed on November 10, 1876.

Visitors climbed stairs inside the Statue of Liberty's arm and smiled for pictures at the top! This photo was taken in 1876.

Another Big Birthday

Many U.S. cities celebrated America's two-hundredth birthday on July 4, 1976. In New York City, 212 ships from 34 countries sailed up the Hudson River. Washington, D.C., had the country's largest fireworks display. About 25,000 people visited Independence Hall in Philadelphia. This was where the Declaration of Independence was first read publicly, in 1776. In Sheboygan, Wisconsin, people tossed 1,776 Frisbees into the air. They chose this number to **represent** the year America declared its independence from Britain.

On July 4, 1976, the Statue of Liberty was surrounded by exploding red, white, and blue fireworks. ▶

Fourth of July Fireworks

Fireworks have been a **tradition** on July 4 since the colonists declared their freedom from Britain. During the war that followed, the colonists didn't have money for fireworks. However, military ships fired rockets over the water on Independence Day. Today's fireworks are quite fancy. They explode into different shapes and colors. Some look like spinning red, white, and blue wheels. Others are showers of stars. The noise and smoke remind people of the war that the colonists fought for America's independence.

◀ *Colorful fireworks exploded above Missouri's St. Louis Gateway Arch on July 4, 1988.*

The Liberty Bell

Certain **symbols** are connected with Independence Day. The Liberty Bell is a well-known symbol of American independence. This bell was made for Pennsylvania's State House, known today as Independence Hall. The bell was made in Britain in 1752.

The Liberty Bell rang to announce important events. Although the exact wording of the Declaration of Independence was decided on July 4, it wasn't adopted until July 7, 1776. On July 8, 1776, the bell rang out that a new nation was born.

The Liberty Bell weighs 2,000 pounds (907 kg). The bell cracked the first time it was rung. It was repaired but it cracked again! ▶

Other July Fourth Symbols

The American flag is a major symbol of Independence Day. On July 4, it flies from even more business buildings and homes than usual. The flag is also carried in parades. It represents freedom. The flag stands for the government, the land, and the people of the United States. The bald eagle, America's national bird, is another regular sight on Independence Day. The bald eagle decorates banners in Independence Day parades. The bald eagle also appears on American coins, dollar bills, and postage stamps.

◀ *The bald eagle became the national bird of the United States in 1782. It stands for the strength and independence of America.*

Celebrating Independence Day

Parades are a big part of Independence Day celebrations. People also show love for their country with **patriotic** speeches and songs. Many people go to a picnic or a barbecue with family and friends. At night people light up their streets and backyards with firecrackers and sparklers. Others go to see fireworks displays in their town or city. The most important part of the celebration is to remember and honor the birth of the United States and the people who fought for its independence.

Glossary

adopted (uh-DOPT-ed) To have accepted or approved something.

American Revolution (uh-MER-uh-ken reh-vuh-LOO-shun) Battles that soldiers from the colonies fought against Britain for freedom, from 1775 to 1783.

celebrate (SEH-luh-brayt) To observe a special time with festivities.

Continental Congress (kon-tin-EN-tul KON-gres) A group, made up of a few people from every colony, that made decisions for the colonies.

Declaration of Independence (deh-kluh-RAY-shun UV in-duh-PEN-dints) A paper, signed on July 4, 1776, declaring that the American colonies were free from British rule.

loyal (LOY-ul) Faithful to a person or an idea.

participated (par-TIH-suh-payt-ed) To have taken part in something.

patriotic (pay-tree-AH-tik) Showing love for one's country.

pursuit (pur-SOOT) The act of trying to get or to seek something.

represent (reh-prih-ZENT) To stand for.

Statue of Liberty (STA-choo UV LIH-bur-tee) A large statue that stands for liberty, located on Liberty Island in New York Harbor.

symbols (SIM-bulz) Objects or designs that stand for something important.

tradition (truh-DIH-shun) A way of doing something that has been passed down over time.

Index

Web Sites

Due to the changing nature of Internet links, PowerKids Press has developed an online list of Web sites related to the subject of this book. This site is updated regularly. Please use this link to access the list:
www.powerkidslinks.com/lhol/independ/